100% UNOFFICIAL GUIDE TO FORTNITE:

A CENTUM BOOK 978-1-913865-81-8
Published in Great Britain by Centum Books Ltd
This edition published 2021
1 3 5 7 9 10 8 6 4 2

Text and design © Centum Books | Images © Shutterstock & © Istock
Additional text and images are reproduced with permission from Cherry Lake
Publishing Group, 2395 South Huron Parkway, Suite 200, Ann Arbor, MI48104, USA
cherrylakepublishing.com

Produced by The Wonderful Ideas Project LTD with
Chris Caulfield (Words) and Nathan Balsom (Art).
Special consultants: Beau Chance, Elijah Caulfield,
Will Shepherd, Dylan & Brody Cardell

Centum Books Ltd, 20 Devon Square,
Newton Abbot, Devon, TQ12 2HR, UK &
9/10 Fenian St, Dublin 2, D02 RX24, Ireland
books@centumbooksltd.co.uk

CENTUM BOOKS Limited Reg. No 07641486

A CIP catalogue record for this book is
available from the British Library.

Printed in China

100% UNOFFICIAL GUIDE TO
FORTNITE

THIS BOOK BELONGS TO

Callum Md

CONTENTS

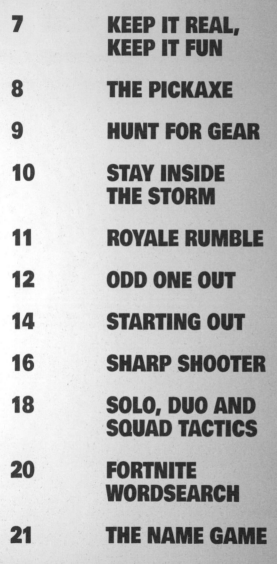

KEEP IT REAL, KEEP IT FUN

IT'S THE PRO'S SKILL, NOT THEIR GEAR, THAT MAKES THEM GREAT.

There are few things as exciting as showing your friends you've reached max level by wearing extremely rare gear, skins or emotes. Just don't let the chase take over your life. Remember, new cool stuff is always being added to Fortnite.

CHARACTER CUSTOMISATION IS AWESOME BUT IT WILL NEVER CHANGE HOW FORTNITE PLAYS. DON'T LET ANYONE TELL YOU OTHERWISE.

We play games to enjoy ourselves and have fun. Fortnite brings people together. Never let anything get in the way of that. There is no need for jealousy or spending more than you can afford. Customisation is a bonus. The real joy comes from honing your skills, winning matches and playing with friends.

THE PICKAXE

As well as being the most basic close-combat weapon in the game (warning: you will want to upgrade this IMMEDIATELY), the pickaxe allows you to smash and grab any object you find. Use it to help gather all those precious materials needed to build your way to the top.

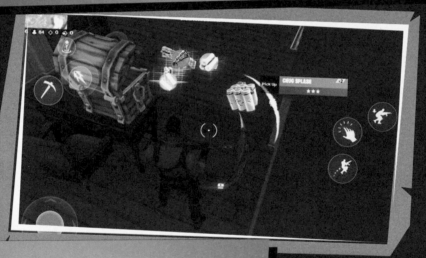

Some harvesting tools can be earned as you play. They look like their real-life counterparts, so expect to find plenty of hammers, axes and crowbars. Fortnite being Fortnite though, expect to also find plenty of weird and wonderful shapes from lollipops to wands, and everything in between.

WE'VE HIDDEN PICKAXES THROUGHOUT YOUR FORTNITE ANNUAL. CAN YOU FIND THEM ALL? HINT, YOU MAY HAVE ALREADY PASSED A FEW.

HUNT FOR GEAR

COMPLETE THIS GRID USING THE SIX PIECES OF GEAR BELOW. EACH ROW AND COLUMN SHOULD CONTAIN ONE OF EACH ITEM.

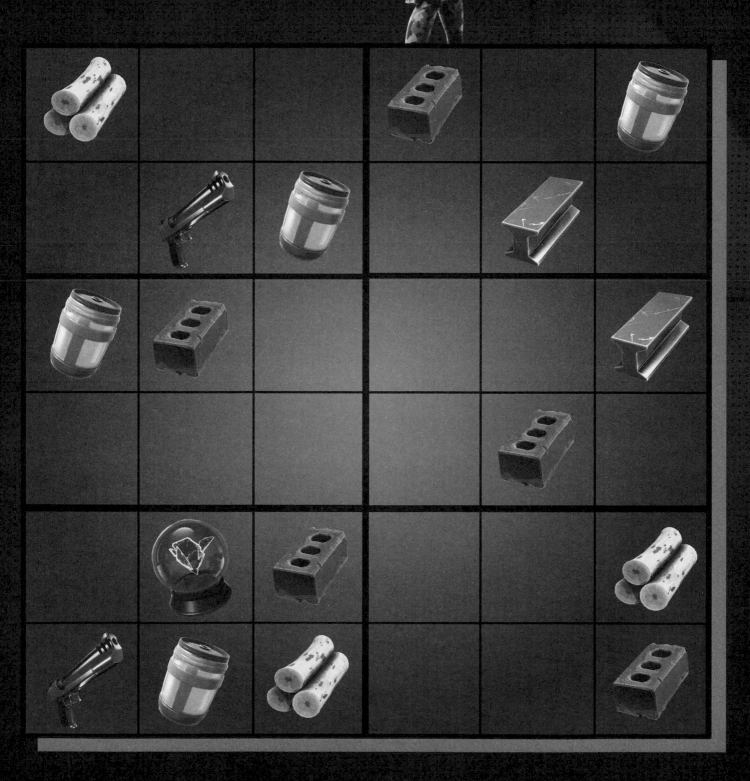

9

Answers on page 44

STAY INSIDE THE *STORM*

DANGER!

The timer has ticked down and you need to get to the final circle without taking any further damage. Only one Fortnite soldier can make it to the middle without running back into the deadly storm. Can you follow the paths taken by Raven, Astro Jack, Blaze, Peely and Midas to work out who grabs the Victory Royale?

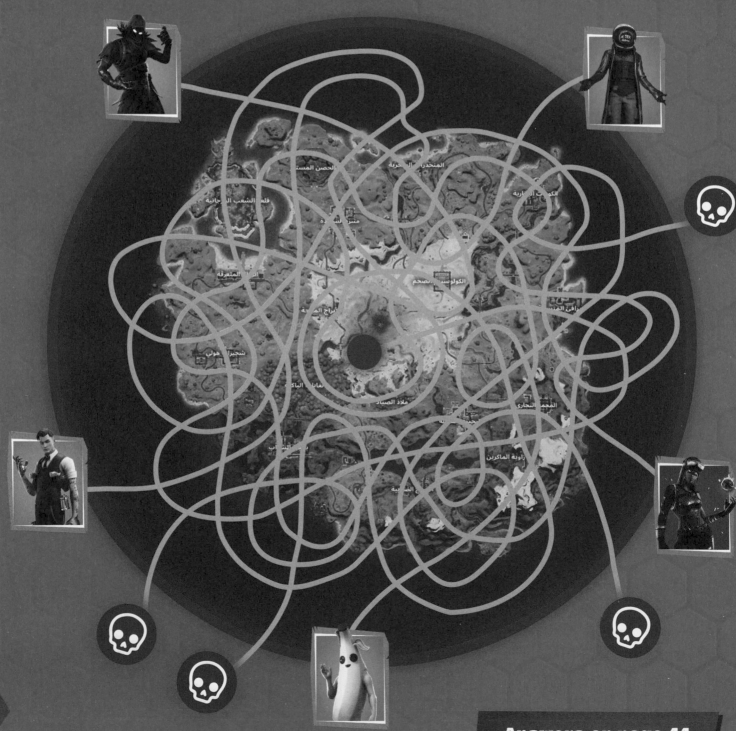

Answers on page 44

ROYALE RUMBLE

THE VIVID COLOURS ON THE SCREEN SCREAM ONE THING - IT'S THE FAST-PACED, FREEFORM, WORLD-BUILDING MULTIPLAYER MAYHEM SHOOTER UNLIKE ANYTHING YOU'VE PLAYED BEFORE.

IT'S BATTLE ROYALE!

READY UP

THE GOAL IS SIMPLE.
BE THE LAST ONE STANDING.

Your mission, and you'll want to accept it, is to load up on weapons, grab some great gear, and make sure you come out on top. So get on the battle bus, start the party, and skydive to your landing spot.

You may feel like a noob surrounded by overpowered superheroes but, armed with your 100% Unofficial Fortnite Annual, you might just score that precious

Victory Royale!

ODD ONE OUT

A SNIPER'S EYE IS NEEDED TO PICK OUT THE ONE IMPOSTER LURKING INSIDE EACH SUPER SQUAD BELOW. ONE CHARACTER IN EVERY PICTURE HAS HAD A SMALL CHANGE THAT MAKES THEM DIFFERENT TO THE ORIGINAL LINE UP. CAN YOU FIND ALL FOUR ODD ONES OUT?

ORIGINAL LINE UP

1

2

3

4

STARTING OUT

WHEN YOU FIRST ARRIVE ON THE ISLAND, YOU'LL BE ARMED WITH JUST YOUR **TRUSTY PICKAXE**. IF YOU WANT TO SURVIVE FOR MORE THAN FIVE MINUTES, YOU NEED TO UPGRADE YOUR WEAPONS, FAST.

Going up against heavily armed opponents will end badly, more often than not.

GRAB THE FIRST GUN YOU SEE, NO MATTER WHAT IT IS. IF YOU CAN'T SHOOT BACK, YOU ARE A SITTING DUCK.

If you are unlucky enough to land where no loot is lying around, find and head inside your nearest building. Remember you only have your harvesting tool at this stage, so will need to be extra careful as you scavenge the rooms for something, anything. **You can't afford to be picky.**

FORTUNATELY THE WORLD OF FORTNITE IS LITTERED WITH WEAPONRY, IT'S PART OF WHAT MAKES IT SUCH A GREAT GAME. SO IT WON'T BE LONG UNTIL YOU'RE ROCKING SOMETHING MUCH MORE POWERFUL!

ONE SUPER TIP:

Not all weapons are created equal. Grey guns are the most common in Fortnite. They will get you started, but you want to keep your eyes peeled for better kit. Look for green, blue and purple guns.

COMMON
UNCOMMON
RARE
EPIC
LEGENDARY
MYTHIC

Some of the rarest weapons you will find are the **legendary golds** and **mythic yellows**. If you are fortunate enough to stumble across an RPG or SCAR assault rifle, do not pass it up, these are incredibly powerful weapons designed to wreak havoc.

TOP TIP

YOU CAN SEE HOW MUCH DAMAGE YOUR WEAPONS DO BY PRESSING 'UP' ON MOST CONTROLLERS TO ACCESS YOUR INVENTORY.

YOU'RE NOW ON YOUR WAY TO BECOMING A ONE-PLAYER ARMY.

SHARP SHOOTER

CAN YOU SPOT THE TEN DIFFERENCES BETWEEN THESE TWO PICTURES?

TEST YOUR NO-SCOPE SKILLS

ANSWERS ON PAGE 44

SOLO, DUO AND SQUAD TACTICS

TOP TIPS TO HELP YOU WIN!

#1 **Find yourself a weapon.** Don't be picky. Without one you will be extremely vulnerable to any other player you come across.

#2 **Be quiet!** If your enemy detects you first, they have the advantage. Running is loud. Walk or crouch when you can.

#3 **Want to hear the enemy?** Headphones will give you the best chance, and help you know where the sound is coming from.

#4 **Stay inside the circle,** away from the storm. When the timer ticks down, being on the inside is key.

#5
Drink shield potions when you get them. You can get your shield to 100 by drinking two smalls and a regular, in that order.

#6
Don't take on an enemy unless you are sure you will win. Remember, the goal is to survive until the end.

#7
When playing in duos or squads, communication is key. Let your friends know what supplies you have and call for backup.

#8
A team that lands together, fights and survives together. Use landmarks to identify targets and all aim for the same spot.

#9
Master building. It is a key tactic used by the pros. In some cases, throwing up quick walls can act as infinite shields.

#10
Don't loot victims straightaway. Gunfights draw attention and everybody can see that attractive pile of fallen stash lying there.

FORTNITE WORDSEARCH

GREAT FORTNITE PLAYERS CAN SPOT THEIR ENEMIES A MILE OFF
AND KNOW WHERE TO LOOK IN ORDER TO DIG OUT THE BEST LOOT.
PUT YOUR SKILLS TO THE TEST WITH THIS WORDSEARCH.

```
R O Y A L E V A C H J G H L B
Q O V B M A T E R I A L S J A
E K C D C F C G L I D E R K T
T F W K R O B D C K K G B H T
G E D R E R U C H U G J U G L
D R I T A T V S C A V E N G E
S G O U T N L G V S I B N G B
P H F M I I O A K N T V T J U
I I O R V T O H U V H O R H S
O R C T E E T J H N G R R G H
B V N K G N B J G B C F A M G
C U I E A U G G Y F D H A F G
K Y T S J X N H T S D S E S H
O U E D H M E G S N I P E R K
B U I L D I N G I K L H G F C
```

FORTNITE ROYALE ROCKET LAUNCHER
SHOTGUN BUILDING BATTLE BUS
STORM CREATIVE SNIPER
SCAVENGE GLIDER PICKAXE
MATERIALS CHUG JUG LOOT

ANSWERS ON PAGE 45

THE **NAME** GAME

CREATE YOUR OWN UNIQUE FORTNITE CHARACTER NAME BY COMBINING THE WORD BESIDE THE FIRST LETTER OF YOUR FIRST NAME AND THE WORD BESIDE THE FIRST LETTER OF YOUR SURNAME.

FIND THE FIRST LETTER OF YOUR FIRST NAME:

A = GIANT	F = SNEAKY	K = FLOSSY	Q = HILARIOUS	V = ROYAL
B = SPIKEY	G = MYSTERIOUS	L = AWESOME	R = SUPER	W = LUCKY
C = CURIOUS	H = GIFTED	M = CLUMSY	S = POWERFUL	X = CLEVER
D = TINY	I = BRAVE	N = STINKY	T = COOL	Y = MEGA
E = AMAZING	J = RICH	O = ITCHY	U = UNRULY	Z = VICTORIOUS
		P = FURRY		

FIND THE FIRST LETTER OF YOUR SURNAME:

A = CAT	F = KNIGHT	K = PIZZA	Q = TREE	V = HERO
B = NERD	G = LLAMA	L = UNICORN	R = ARTIST	W = MUSHROOM
C = GNOME	H = VOYAGER	M = STAR	S = BEAR	X = BANANA
D = MOUSE	I = SHARK	N = TANK	T = DANCER	Y = JOKER
E = FIGHTER	J = BOULDER	O = EAGLE	U = WARRIOR	Z = BALLOON
		P = TURTLE		

MY FORTNITE CHARACTER NAME IS:

Curious   Star

BUILD FOR VICTORY

PANIC WALL

Great for grabbing those crucial added seconds to duck behind while you reload, heal, or just straight up flee.

PANIC RAMP

A quickly built ramp during close combat wi get you above your opponent or help you duck out of sight for even more protection.

V-SHAPED RAMP

Panic ramps with two sets of stairs opposite each other to form a 'V'. At the top of towers they create perfect vantage points.

SNIPER TOWER

Box yourself in with walls then add a ramp to move higher up. Repeat to build a skyscraper, now add a V-shaped ramp.

TOP TIP

The stronger the building material in your base, the harder it is to shoot it down - and send you tumbling to your doom.

HEALING ROOM

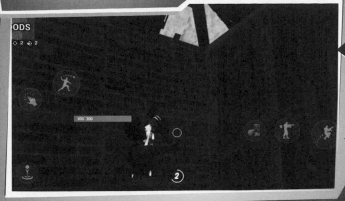

A place to hide and heal. Surround yourself with four walls and a roof for those precious extra seconds to med up.

WARNING:

Launch pads must be placed on a floor tile and for goodness sake build them away from trees or buildings.

WARNING:

Healing Rooms stand out and attract attention so don't linger too long otherwise they will quickly turn into hurt lockers.

LAUNCH PAD

Epic rare item that hurls you into the air so you can use your glider to quickly escape enemy attacks or the oncoming storm.

BOUNCER TRAP

Used to launch players off high places such as mountains or sniper towers while avoiding fall damage.

DAMAGE TRAP

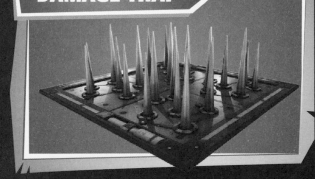

Best placed inside a house or fort for unsuspecting players to stumble across, or dropped on your rivals.

COZY CAMPFIRE

Healed two hit points per second for 25 seconds. Sharing these was a surefire way to become popular.

TOP TIP

Build a door at the bottom of your tower with a trap inside it and revel in your victim's downfall as they try to sneak after you.

BOUNTY HUNTER

ONE WAY TO BECOME A FORTNITE MASTER IS TO HONE YOUR SKILLS WITH A SERIES OF TESTS.

Try each of the challenge cards and record how you have done to chart your progress. Some are as much about learning as they are about winning.

Get an adult to help you cut carefully around the dotted lines of the cards opposite and then shuffle the deck, before randomly selecting a different challenge to accept. **Ready up soldier!.**

	DIFFICULTY RATING	TIME TAKEN	ATTEMPTS MADE
1			
2			
3			
4			
5			
6			
7			
8			
9			

1

PEACE CORPS

SELF-DEFENCE ONLY
SHOOT WHEN SHOT AT

2

PISTOLS AT DAWN

YOU CAN ONLY PICK UP
AND USE PISTOLS

3

MATERIALISM

TRY TO PLAY
WITHOUT BUILDING
ANYTHING

4

ROWDY RACKET

NO CROUCHING
OR WALKING. RUN
EVERYWHERE

5

WHO NEEDS BUILDINGS?

YOU ARE NOT
ALLOWED INSIDE
ANY STRUCTURES

6

ILL COMMUNICATION

NO HEADSETS. YOU
CANNOT TALK WITH
ANY OTHER PLAYERS

7

LOOT IS FOR LOSERS

YOU CAN NOT PICK
UP ANY ITEMS SO
PICKAXES ONLY FOLKS

8

POTION MASTER

NO CHUG JUGS OR
ANY KIND OF MEDS

9

SPY MODE

SILENCED
WEAPONS ONLY

BOUNTY HUNTER PACK

BOUNTY HUNTER PACK

BOUNTY HUNTER PACK

BOUNTY HUNTER PACK

BOUNTY HUNTER PACK

BOUNTY HUNTER PACK

BOUNTY HUNTER PACK

BOUNTY HUNTER PACK

FACT OR FICTION ?

PERFECT AIM AND BUILDING SKILLS ARE IMPRESSIVE ON THE BATTLEFIELDS OF FORTNITE BUT IN THE PLAYGROUND, KNOWLEDGE IS KING.

Test your understanding of the epic shooter with this fun true or false quiz. Once you've solved them yourself, why not try them on your friends?

#2 THE MORE MONEY YOU SPEND ON YOUR CHARACTER, THE BETTER THEY PERFORM IN THE GAME.

#1 FORTNITE IS PLAYED BY 200,000,000 (TWO HUNDRED MILLION) PLAYERS AROUND THE WORLD.

#4 FORTNITE EARNED ABOUT ₤2 BILLION IN 2018.

#3 BATTLE ROYALE WAS NOT SUPPOSED TO BE FORTNITE'S CALLING CARD.

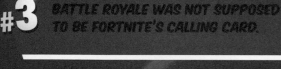

#5 THE BEST WAY TO WIN AT FORTNITE IS TO CHEAT.

#6 FORTNITE WAS RUSHED OUT TO CASH IN ON THE GROWING POPULARITY OF ONLINE GAMING.

#7 YOU CAN PLAY FORTNITE WITH AND AGAINST YOUR FRIENDS NO MATTER WHAT SYSTEM THEY ARE PLAYING ON, EVEN IF IT'S DIFFERENT FROM YOURS.

#8 FORTNITE IS THE MOST STREAMED GAME ON TWITCH.

#9 THERE IS A FORTNITE WORLD CUP AND IT HAS A PRIZE POOL OF ABOUT ₤25 MILLION.

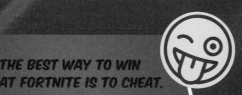

#10 THE RECON EXPERT SKIN IS FAMOUS BECAUSE IT IS SO RARE.

ANSWERS ON PAGE 45

TOP 10 SKINS OF ALL TIME

★★★★★

DO YOU AGREE?

TOMATOHEAD

Classic fruit-on-head character. First released in Season 3 as part of the Pizza Pit Set.

P.A.N.D.A.

Legendary Outfit from Season 5. Keep an eye out for the limited edition Valentine Pink Bear.

FISHSTICK

A big hit since its Season 7 release. Fishstick even became the mascot of its own restaurant in the Craggy Hills.

GUFF

From the Chapter 2 Season 2 Mythical Might set, but your guess is as good as anybody else's as to what Guff is.

RAVEN

The mysterious Legendary skin from Season 3. Ravens are often associated with prophecies and insight.

PEELY

A reward for reaching Tier 47 of the Season 8 Battle Pass, Peely's popularity rivals that of Fishstick.

Those lucky enough to reach Level 100 in Chapter 2 were rewarded with this nifty villain.

MIDAS

Believe it or not this Slurp Squad hero is a friendly blob made of, you guessed it, slurp.

RIPPLEY

ASTRO JACK

Space-themed skin added in Chapter 2 Season 2. Pulses and glows when dancing.

BLAZE

Not to be confused with the Glider that shares its name. This came out in Chapter 2 Season 3 with the Lava Series.

KNOW YOUR WEAPONS

YOU'VE GOT YOUR FIRST WEAPON. THAT'S GREAT, DON'T STOP THERE.

Every weapon in Fortnite has its use, but if you are just beginning, look out for assault rifles and submachine guns. These are the most useful weapons, in most situations.

Snipers are for crack shots, shotguns rule at close quarters. Once you've got to grips with the basics, our weapons guide will have you firing on all cylinders.

SHOTGUNS

Keep a shotgun for close-up duels as few match their phenomenal stopping power. They often only need one shot to drop an opponent.

Shotguns typically come in heavy, pump or tactical forms, with other models making appearances depending on the season or game mode. Each has its own stats and feel but be careful as they have slow rates of fire, limited magazines, and long reload times.

Look out for the **ultra-rare Dragon's Breath** that fires every single shell at the same time and causes wooden buildings to catch fire. **OUCH!**

PISTOLS

Small, one-handed weapons that are often seen as a 'better than nothing' option.

They can be useful at medium range, away from the deadly blasts of shotguns, and can do considerable damage per second, but, and it is A BIG BUT, they carry so few rounds you will be reloading in the middle of a lot of gunfights.

Some pistols are 'suppressed' - the technical term for silenced - useful for players who like to surprise their foes.

SNIPER RIFLES

The best way to stay alive in Fortnite is to steer clear of your enemies. The best way to knock them off at a distance, is with a sniper rifle.

Just make sure you have anything else to hand for when you get swarmed because snipers are next to useless up close.

Sniper rifles are powerful enough to bring enemies down in a single shot but have small magazines, slow rates of fire, and long reload times.

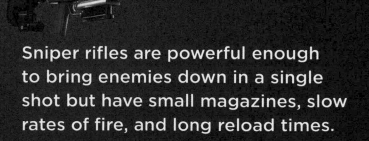

EXPLOSIVE WEAPONS

When the time comes to blow everything up, you will want to reach for a grenade or rocket launcher.

They are the perfect endgame weapons, especially when enemies are clustered together and the building bonanza has begun. These weapons can dish out devastating damage over a wide area.

The damage from the explosion is often enough to wipe out your opponents but don't waste your shots as ammo is in short supply and they are slow to reload.

TOP TIP

If you suspect a tower is packed with rival players, don't waste time trying to pick them off one by one. Use a grenade or rocket launcher to bring down the whole structure, taking everyone inside with it.

MELEE WEAPONS

If you've read this far you must really want to know everything there is about Fortnite's weapons and we salute you. However, Melee weapons should come with a health warning, yours! If you want something slow and weak you are in luck. They are called 'harvesting tools' for a reason. Best to find something, anything, quickly.

ASSAULT WEAPONS

This is more like it. Assault rifles are your workhorse medium-range machines that can still do a decent job close up or further away if you don't have anything better.

They can hold large magazines and fire very quickly, making them the perfect all-rounder, particularly if you are just starting out and haven't yet mastered all the weapons in Fortnite.

Assault weapons come in three main forms, standard, tactical, and heavy, each differing in damage and fire rates. In some game modes you can even add scopes to certain rifles and use them like snipers.

SUBMACHINE GUNS

Submachine guns (or SMGs to those in the know) are great rapid-fire weapons designed to hurl bullets across a wide area.

Think of them as insect swarms dealing out vast amounts of small damage that soon adds up. The tough part isn't hitting your opponent, because you certainly will, the skill is hitting them enough times to stop them in their tracks.

You can even find 'suppressed' SMGs to make a great pairing with any of your spy skins.

BONUS TIP

All weapons handle and fire differently. When starting out, use the ones you feel most comfortable with and practise with them. Learn their recoil patterns and how many shots they need to take out your enemies.

GET SET, SHOOT

A FORTNITE PRO ALWAYS CARRIES THE RIGHT TOOL FOR THE JOB.

By now you should be well on your way to learning about all the different weapons in Fortnite. So let's put that knowledge to the test.

Below are **three important missions** that call for a **special super soldier.** Are you ready for the challenge?

- Follow your orders for each of the missions

- All missions require you to start at the square marked X on the map

- Whichever square your mission takes you to, is your firing position

- Choose the right weapon depending on your distance from the mission target

- Select either the close-up shotgun, a mid-range assault rifle, or the sniper rifle for long-distance shots

Target A :

Move five squares west, go eight squares south, sneak through two squares east, sprint four squares north, march one square east. You should be able to see the enemy. What weapon do you use?

Target B :

Move four squares south, go five squares west, run north for two squares to avoid enemy fire, swim for one square west. You can't get any closer, now's your chance, what weapon do you use?

Target C :

Sneak eight squares south fast. Then you will need to move quietly west for three squares. Now make your way north for one square and take out the enemy. What weapon do you think would be best?

FOLLOW THE INSTRUCTIONS ON PAGE 34, MARK WHERE YOU ARE SENT, AND THEN PICK YOUR WEAPON TO TAKE OUT YOUR TARGET.

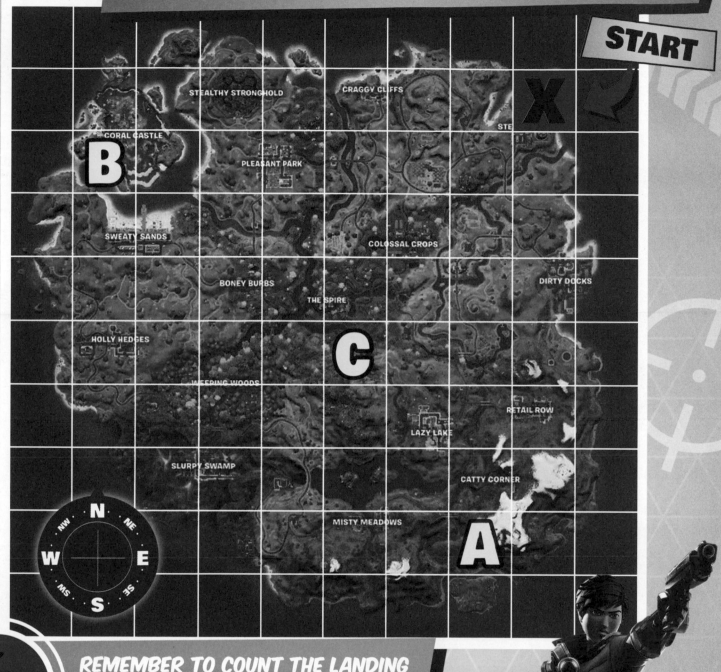

START

STEALTHY STRONGHOLD · CRAGGY CLIFFS · X · STE
CORAL CASTLE · B
PLEASANT PARK
SWEATY SANDS · COLOSSAL CROPS
BONEY BURBS · DIRTY DOCKS
THE SPIRE
HOLLY HEDGES · C
WEEPING WOODS
RETAIL ROW
LAZY LAKE
SLURPY SWAMP · CATTY CORNER
MISTY MEADOWS · A

Compass: N, NE, E, SE, S, SW, W, NW

REMEMBER TO COUNT THE LANDING SPOT AS YOUR FIRST SQUARE!

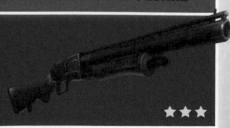

SHOTGUN
SHORT RANGE: ONE SQUARE
★★★

ASSAULT RIFLE
MEDIUM RANGE: TWO SQUARES
★★★★

SNIPER RIFLE
LONG RANGE: THREE SQUARES
★★★★★

Answers on page 45

LEGENDARY, MYTHIC
AND JUST PLAIN GREAT WEAPONS

The SCAR

Ask a Fortnite veteran what's the best weapon and most will say the SCAR assault rifle. This ultra-dependable favourite deals out nearly 200 damage per shot. It's equally lethal over long distances as close up.

Jules' Drum Gun

The 40-round magazine means you can let the bullets fly freely. Eliminate Jules at The Authority and his gun is yours. Those extra shots make it ace at taking out towers. What's not to love?

Ocean's Burst Assault Rifle

What's better than hitting somebody with one shot. Two of course! The Ocean fires a two-burst pulse and its 222 damage per second puts this up there with some of the best in the game's history.

Bolt Action Sniper Rifle

Practice makes perfect but **OMG** is it worth it. Few weapons in Fortnite reward patience and effort as much as the bolt action sniper. Get your aim right and you're an unstoppable long-range player.

HINT: LEARN THE RECOIL PATTERNS OF YOUR RAPID-FIRE WEAPONS SO YOU KNOW WHERE TO AIM THAT FIRST SHOT

TOP TIP

Remember, over distances gravity has an effect on your shots. Aim just above where you want your shot to land.

Tactical Shotgun

As much a dream for you, as a nightmare for anybody foolish enough to stand in your way. A perfectly named weapon, if your tactics are to leap about, building and moving, while spamming the trigger.

Infinity Blade

Overpowered mythic melee weapon. Players would slash at their enemies, quickly cutting them down, and could destroy the environment in a single blow. Unsurprisingly, it was soon vaulted.

Rocket Launcher

Long-time players will remember rocket launchers with fondness for their tower-toppling prowess. These are fort-destroying machines that suit long-range battles, unless you're happy blowing yourself up too? Kaboom!

Minigun

If you want to use this master of disaster you'll need to hop over to Creative mode. But believe us, it's worth stepping away from Battle Royale for the opportunity to witness its devastating fire power.

Compact SMG

When you want to wipe out an entire room full of rivals, look no further. Use a compact SMG at close range and its spray-n-pray characteristics will spread panic wider than the bullets it spews.

Dragon's Breath Shotgun

This sinister serpent spits all four of its rounds at once, covering a vast area and causing massive damage. Want more? How about it also burns anything it hits so be careful it doesn't come back to bite you.

Last one standing. Jonesy is hiding and it is up to you to find him to claim top spot and a glorious Victory Royale. Using your sniper skills, can you scan this picture and locate the sneaky soldier's hiding spot?

Answer on page 45

DO YOU KNOW YOUR WEAPONS?

You need to be fully equipped to take on all comers in Fortnite so let's make sure you know your pistols and rifles from your rockets.

ANSWER THESE SEVEN TOUGH PUZZLERS AND PROVE YOU'RE READY FOR THE BATTLE ROYALE!

 #1 Name a small one-handed weapon that can get you out of a jam and can be good at helping you go undetected.

 #2 Who needs to aim when you're carrying one of these heavy weapons? Just fire in the general direction and go win.

 #3 You can aim down the scope and pick off your enemies from across the map with this beauty.

 #4 Running around with the trigger pulled, firing bullets in every direction is the way to go with this weapon.

 #5 Not all weapons are guns, some have pins that you pull before being thrown.

 #6 The ultimate short-range blaster that can take down your opponent in just one shot.

 #7 Not only are these the best all-round weapon types, but some would argue the super-rare version is the best weapon in the game.

40

Answers on page 45

IMPORTANCE OF BUILDING

YOU THOUGHT FORTNITE WAS A SHOOTING GAME? THINK AGAIN. FORTNITE IS BUILDING FIRST, EVERYTHING ELSE IS SECOND.

WHAT SEPARATES THE BEST FROM THE REST ISN'T THEIR AIM, IT'S HOW QUICKLY AND EFFICIENTLY THEY BUILD. LUCKILY, THIS BOOK HAS YOU COVERED.

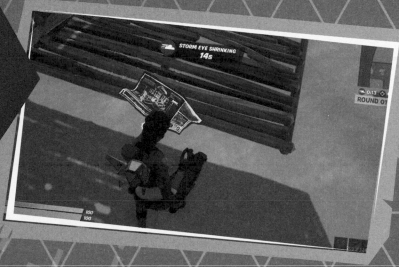

TOP TIP

Change your controller settings. Don't stick with the default layout. Switch to Builder Pro to give your construction skills an instant boost.

As the name suggests, Builder Pro will turn you into a building expert helping your speed and accuracy.

Activate Builder Pro by going to 'Settings' and selecting 'Builder Pro' under 'Configuration'.

Learning to build helps you get to higher ground and those hard-to-reach places. This gives you a vital advantage. It lets you fire downwards on your enemies giving you a bigger target area, and that means **MORE DAMAGE**.

HOW TO FLOSS

IF THERE IS ONE DANCE PEOPLE LINK WITH FORTNITE, IT'S THE FLOSS. THE CRAZY ARM-SWINGY DANCE HAS BEEN PERFORMED THE WORLD OVER BY COUNTLESS CELEBRITIES, SPORTS STARS, AND OF COURSE, SCHOOL KIDS.

Those new to flossing however, may wonder where or how to get in on the act; the dance is no longer available in Fortnite. If you were there, you were there.

Fear not, 100% Fortnite Unofficial guide has you covered. Just follow these easy steps and you'll be flossing the night away with the best of them.

#1
Stand with your feet shoulder-width apart. With your arms straight by your side, make fists with your hands like you're holding a rope, or dental floss, geddit?

#2
Keeping your arms straight, swing them both to your left. As you are doing this, push your hips to the right. If you can get both fists past your hips you're doing great!

#3
Swing your arms to the right and hips to the left but this time keep your left arm in front of your body, and right arm behind you. This is the 'behind' move.

#4
This next one shouldn't be that tricky. You just undo step 3 so that you are back to stage two! See how the arms are basically in the the same position as before.

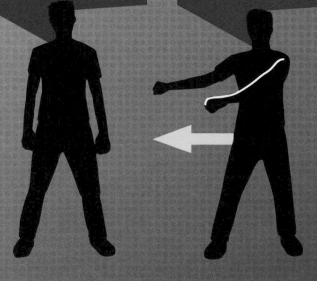

The tricky part is stitching it together. But if you can swing your arms one way and your hips the other, you'll get the hang of it in no time.

To help you visualise, think: 'Why is this dance called The Floss?'. You will get quicker with practice, and the faster you can do it, the cooler it looks.

THE KEY THINGS TO REMEMBER ARE:

Swing your hips side to side and 'back, forward, change' with your arms. Put them together and you've got the Floss.

TO BEGIN, JUST MOVE YOUR HIPS FROM SIDE TO SIDE.

NOW THE ARMS. REMEMBER: BACK, FORWARD, CHANGE.

TOP TIP

With practice you can start with your arms to the right to make your Floss even more impressive.

#5

Now it's time for the 'forward' stage. Simply swing your arms across the front of your body, with your hips going the other way. You need to floss both sides.

#6

Almost there! Time for another 'behind' but this time when you swing your arms to the left, keep your right arm in front of you and your left arm tucked behind.

#7

Last step, don't give up now! Swing your arms back to the right while pushing your hips to the left. Don't look now but **YOU'VE JUST DONE THE FLOSS!**

TOP TIP

Small hip movements make for faster flossing, but if you push them out further your dance will be more dramatic. Have a go at both and see what you like best, or try mixing and matching to make your own style.

ANSWERS

Page 9 **HUNT FOR GEAR**

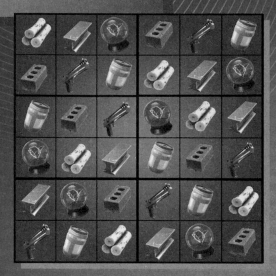

Page 10 **STAY INSIDE THE STORM**

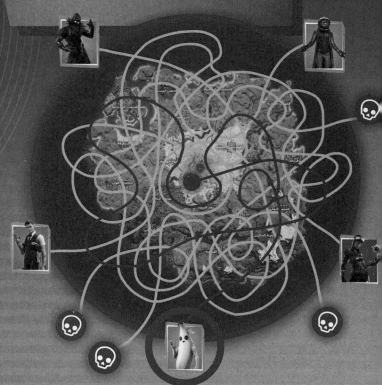

Page 12 **ODD ONE OUT**

1

2

3

4

Page 16
SHARP SHOOTER

Page 20
FORTNITE WORDSEARCH

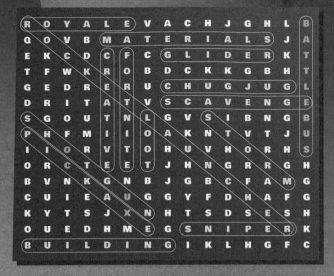

Page 27 FACT OR FICTION?

 #1 FICTION — FORTNITE IS PLAYED BY MORE THAN 350,000,000 PEOPLE. THAT MAKES IT BIGGER THAN NETFLIX.

 #2 FICTION — SKINS AND WRAPS EXIST TO LET YOU MAKE YOUR AVATAR REFLECT YOUR OWN MOOD OR PERSONALITY. THEY DON'T MEAN YOU WILL BE A BETTER PLAYER.

 #3 FACT — FORTNITE WAS DESIGNED TO BE A BUILDING GAME WITH A HORDE MODE. THE BATTLE ROYALE EXPLOSION CAUGHT THE WORLD BY SURPRISE.

 #4 FACT — JUST SHOWS THE AMAZING DRAWING POWER OF A FUN GAME THAT LETS YOUR IMAGINATION RUN WILD AND PROVIDES HAIR-TRIGGER THRILLS.

 #5 FICTION — CHEATERS GET BANNED. THE GAME'S CREATOR HAS EVEN BEEN KNOWN TO TAKE LEGAL ACTION AGAINST PLAYERS SUSPECTED OF CHEATING.

 #6 FICTION — DEVELOPERS EPIC GAMES BEGAN WORKING ON FORTNITE IN 2011, IT DIDN'T GET LAUNCHED UNTIL 2017. NOW, THAT'S DEDICATION!

 #7 FACT — YOU CAN FORM YOUR OWN SUPER SQUADS NO MATTER WHAT PLATFORM YOUR BUDDIES ARE PLAYING ON. HOW COOL IS THAT?!

#8 FACT — AT PEAK TIMES MORE THAN 650,000 AVID FANS TUNE IN TO WATCH FORTNITE STREAMS, MAKING IT MORE POPULAR THAN SOME TV SHOWS.

#9 DOUBLE FACT — THAT'S RIGHT. PLAYERS FIGHT OVER A WHOPPING £25 MILLION PRIZE POOL, WITH A TOP PRIZE OF £2.5M FOR THE BEST SOLO PLAYER.

#10 FACT — IT WAS RELEASED IN OCTOBER 2017 WHEN FEW PEOPLE PAID FOR SKINS. DESPITE ITS SIMPLE LOOK, IF YOU HAVE IT, YOU STAND OUT.

Page 34
GET SET, SHOOT

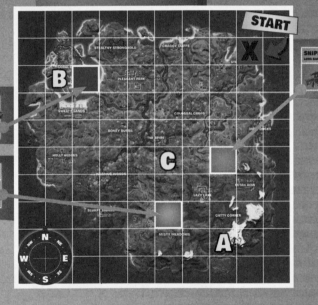

Page 38 WHERE'S JONESY?

Page 40
DO YOU KNOW YOUR WEAPONS?

1. SUPPRESSED PISTOL
2. ROCKET LAUNCHER
3. SNIPER RIFLE
4. SMG
5. GRENADE
6. SHOTGUN
7. ASSAULT RIFLE

HOW DID YOU DO?!

Top Ten Tips for Keeping it Safe and Keeping it Fun!

#1 Never, ever, ever tell anyone your real name – don't use it as your username either!

#2 Don't tell anyone your age, school or address

#3 Don't give out any other personal info – about you, your friends or your family

#4 Your passwords are there to keep you safe – don't share them with anyone (except your parents or carers)

#5 There are lots of websites where you need to be over 13 to create an account. ALWAYS ask your parents or carers for permission before registering for websites

#6 If something doesn't feel right, it probably isn't right. Always share worries with your parents or carers

#7 Always be kind online. If someone is mean to you, tell your parents or carers straightaway. Remember it's always supposed to be fun!

#8 Take lots of breaks from gaming and the screen, the best players know that rests and real-life skills make them better gamers!

#9 It is better to play in shared spaces or close to your parents or carers

#10 Remember you don't need to spend money to have fun online

Note *FORTNITE: BATTLE ROYALE* is rated PEGI 12